DREAM

A True Story of Courage and Determination

BIG

Dave McGillivray, *Boston Marathon Race Director*

with Nancy Feehrer

Illustrated by Ron Himler

"The guy who stands 5-foot-4 dares to stand apart. He challenges others to do the same in their lives, whatever their dreams may be."
—**BARRY SCANLON**, *Lowell Sun*, March 29, 2000

"Physical stature or any other challenge does not need to define you or prevent you from dreaming big and working hard to make those dreams reality."
—**BILL BELICHICK**, head coach of the New England Patriots

"I have grand babies now and am reading a lot of kids' books! This one is superior in its message and originality."
—**DAVE COWENS**, retired NBA player and head coach, elected to the Basketball Hall of Fame

Dedication

This book is dedicated in memory of Joseph Middlemiss, a beloved big dreamer who has influenced and inspired us all, and to his little brother, Jack, who shows us daily what true courage and determination look like.

Acknowledgments

We are grateful to Peter and Paul Reynolds for their generous help and encouragement, and to friends, family members, and astute "official" readers who offered feedback and ideas. Thank you to the 2015–2016 class of third, fourth, and fifth grade writers and artists and the teachers and staff at the Abbot School in Westford, Massachusetts, for helping to inspire and create this book. Finally, thank you to Scott and Kate Middlemiss and The Joseph Middlemiss Big Heart Foundation for your partnership in getting this book into the hands of many deserving kids.

Nomad Press
A division of Nomad Communications
10 9 8 7 6 5 4 3 2 1
Copyright © 2018 by Dave McGillivray. All rights reserved.

This book was manufactured by CGB Printers,
North Mankato, Minnesota, United States
February 2018, Job #240606

ISBN: 978-1-61930-618-9

Questions regarding the ordering of this book should be addressed to
Nomad Press
2456 Christian St.
White River Junction, VT 05001
www.nomadpress.net

Printed in the United States.

When I was little, I was little.
Really little.

But my dreams? They were BIG.

I dreamed of being an athlete. A *professional* athlete.
Someday, I'd shoot hoops for the Celtics,
play second base for the Red Sox, and
score touchdowns for the Patriots.

My dreams were **BIG**, but I was small.
The kids at school never let me forget it. Ever.

When they picked teams at recess,
I was always the last one picked.
And I mean *last*.

I tried out for lots of teams,
but I was never given a chance.

After I tried out for the basketball team,
the coach sighed and shook his head.
"You're a great athlete, Dave.
You're just a little too . . . little."

This gave me an idea.

I ran straight home and up to my room.
With a thick, black permanent marker, I made a sign.

I stuck it over my bed with a little bit of tape
and a lot of hope.

As I got older, I did grow a little bigger,
but not a lot bigger.

When I woke up on my 12th birthday,
I decided to try a new sport: *running*.

No tryouts required.

I laced up my sneakers and ran all the way around
a huge pond near my house. As I rounded the last corner to home,
there was my favorite person in the whole world.

"Grandpa," I panted. "I just ran all the way around Spot Pond!"
"Wow!" he cheered. "That's about 5 or 6 miles, I'd guess."
"Guess what else?" I said. "When I get bigger,
I'm going to be a professional athlete."

"Dave," Grandpa began gently, "sometimes in life, things don't work out
the way you want, and you have to find a different way.
Maybe if you can't *be* big, you can *do* something big."

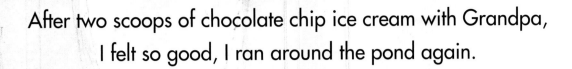

After two scoops of chocolate chip ice cream with Grandpa,
I felt so good, I ran around the pond again.

I ran 12 miles on my 12th birthday.
I had started something big!

On my 13th birthday, I did it again, but I added an extra mile.
On my 14th birthday, I ran 14 miles.
15 on my 15th, 16 on my 16th,
and—you guessed it—
17 miles on my
17th birthday.

All this running inspired another **BIG** dream.
Someday, I'd run the Boston Marathon.

A marathon is a long race—more than 26 miles.
I had never run *that* far before.
But how hard could it be?

So, at age 17, with very little thinking or training
and a borrowed race bib, I decided to run it.

"Grandpa, I'm going to run the Boston Marathon today!"
"Today?" Grandpa asked, surprised. "But, Dave, you haven't
trained for the marathon. Are you sure you're ready?"
"Sure, I'm sure," I replied.

"Tell you what, you do your best, and I'll walk over to
the course and cheer you on," Grandpa promised.
"Deal!" I said. "I'll wave to you as I sprint by!"

There I was at the starting line of the Boston Marathon, 1972.

"Runners! On your mark . . . get set . . ." **BANG!**

The starting gun went off, and off I ran. *Fast.*
I'd been dreaming of this race for a long time.
In my dream, I sprinted across the famous finish line,
breaking the tape, my arms raised in victory.

I just knew I could do it.

(Wow, was I wrong.)

At Mile 18, I collapsed in a heap on the sidewalk.
I couldn't run even one more step.

An officer helped me up and into his police car.
With the lights flashing, he sped me to the hospital.

The doctor said I'd be fine, but I wasn't thinking about me.
All I could think of was Grandpa.
He was probably still out on the race course, waiting.

Later that night, when I was back home, Grandpa called.
"Where were you?" he said. "I was waiting for you."

"I just couldn't do it," I groaned. "I failed."

"No," he said calmly, "you didn't fail.
You discovered something."

"I did?" I asked, rolling my eyes.

"Yes, you discovered that big dreams don't just *come true*.
They take work, *hard work*.
I'll make you a deal. If you train and work hard, I promise
to wait for you next year and cheer you on."

"Deal," I said. "I'll wave to you, Grandpa, as I sprint by."
"Sprint?" Grandpa laughed. "Just finish this time."

I trained every day, running miles and miles to get ready.

Sometimes, though, things don't work out the way you want.

Just two months into my training,
something unimaginable happened.

My Grandpa died.
He wouldn't be waiting for me on the race course.

I decided to keep my end of the deal anyway.
I'd run the Boston Marathon.

This time, though, I'd finish it for him.

The day was finally here for my second Boston Marathon.
I had trained. I had worked hard.
But that morning, I woke up sick.

Sometimes, things *really* don't work out.

"I'm still going to run," I told my worried mom.
"Are you sure?" she asked. "You don't look so good."

"Sure, I'm sure," I whispered.
"I'm running for Grandpa."

16

I didn't feel great, but there I was at the starting line.

"Runners! On your mark . . . get set . . ." **BANG!**
Off I ran, speeding past the Mile 1 marker,
Mile 2 . . . Mile 3 . . .
So far so good, I thought.
My legs and lungs remembered all their training.
Mile 4 . . . Mile 5 . . . Mile 6 . . .
"I wish Grandpa could be here."

Luckily, Mom and Dad were cheering me on.
Mile 7 . . . Mile 8 . . . Mile 9 . . .
My body ached all over, but I kept running.

Mile 10 . . . Mile 11 . . . Mile 12 . . .
Still going. But my feet felt like bricks. Heavy, *sore* bricks.

Mile 13 . . . Mile 14 . . . Mile 15 . . .
"Keep moving!" I said to myself. "Breathe! Breathe!"

Mile 16 . . .

Mile 17 . . .

At Mile 18, my stomach flipped as I remembered
collapsing last year. I jogged s – l – o – w – l – y past.
"You have to finish this race," I told myself.
"This one's for Grandpa."

Mile 19 . . . Mile 20 . . .
But I was so sick, so tired. Every single step hurt.
Mile 21 . . . My legs began to wobble. My head did, too.
"This can't be happening!"

But it was happening.
Partway through Mile 21, I collapsed. Again.
For the second time, I'd let Grandpa down.

What a failure!

I was still little, always picked last for games,
never picked for teams.

My biggest dream was to be a great athlete.

I slumped on the sidewalk—completely defeated.
It was the end of the road for me.
(I guess they call this part of the Boston Marathon
"Heartbreak Hill" for a reason.)

"*Sometimes* in life things don't work out
the way you want?" I sobbed into my hands.
"Really?
How about *all the time* things don't work out!"

Then, I lifted my head and looked around.
Something looked so familiar about this place.

Suddenly, I realized I had collapsed next to Evergreen Cemetery.
Grandpa's cemetery.

Grandpa was waiting for me! He *had* kept his promise—
but in a little different way. There he was, silently cheering me on,
encouraging me to get back in the race.

I scraped myself up off the sidewalk.
Slowly, I began limping, then walking, then jogging.

Grandpa had kept his promise to wait for me.

And I'd keep mine to finish this race.

Mile 22 . . . Mile 23 . . . Mile 24 . . .
His encouragement filled my head as I forced
my legs to make each painful step.

Mile 25 . . . Mile 26 . . .
The crowds! The cheering!
"Keep going!" "You're almost there!" "You can do it!"

Could I? Could I do it?

I could. I DID!
There it was: Mile 26.2

the **FINISH LINE**.

As I stumbled across the finish line,
I threw my arms in the air and gasped,

"Grandpa, we did it!"

Since that day, I've run
every Boston Marathon—every single one.

And guess what? I always come in last.
You see, I used to just run the Boston Marathon, but now
I *run* the Boston Marathon.
I'm the race director.
I make sure everything is ready for more than 30,000 runners.

Each year, after everyone has finished running and I've finished directing,
I go back to the start and run the whole marathon at night.

Partway through mile 21, I always smile
and give a little wave to Grandpa.

I dreamed of being a professional athlete.
And guess what? I am.

I just had to find a different way.

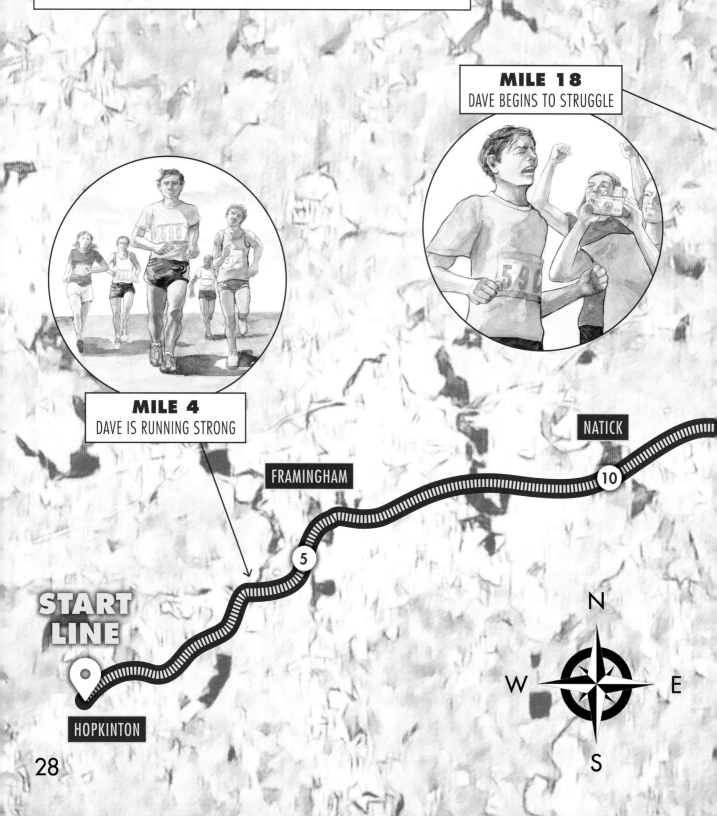

THE BOSTON MARATHON ROUTE

MILE 18
DAVE BEGINS TO STRUGGLE

MILE 4
DAVE IS RUNNING STRONG

NATICK

FRAMINGHAM

10

5

START LINE

HOPKINTON

N
W E
S

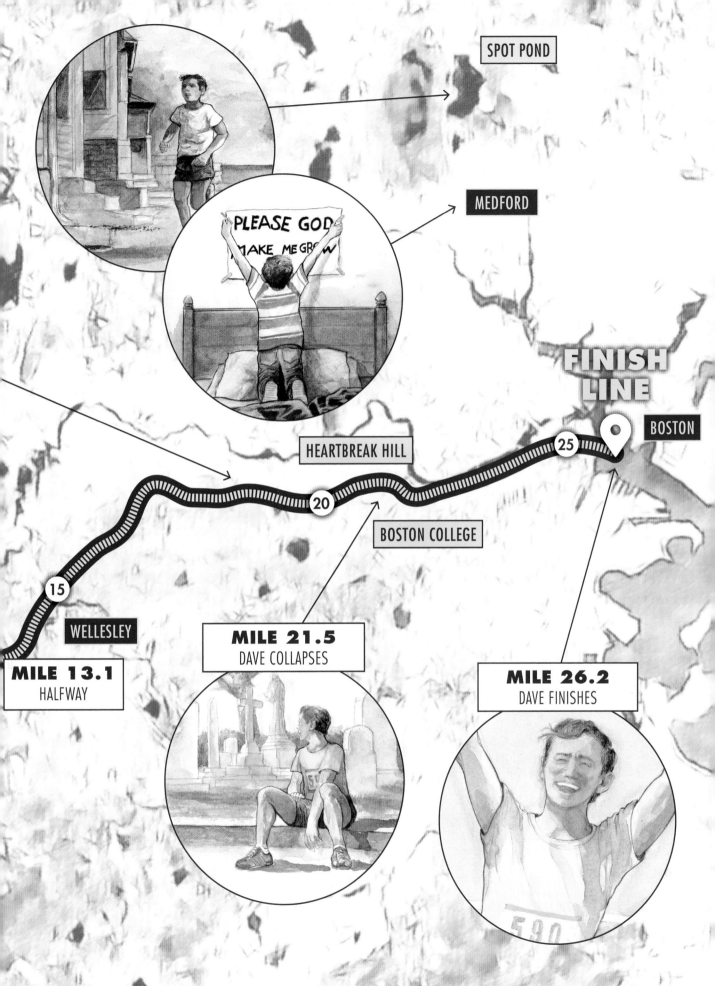

SPOT POND

MEDFORD

PLEASE GOD
MAKE ME GROW

FINISH
LINE

BOSTON

25

HEARTBREAK HILL

20

BOSTON COLLEGE

15

WELLESLEY

MILE 21.5
DAVE COLLAPSES

MILE 13.1
HALFWAY

MILE 26.2
DAVE FINISHES

590

The DREAM BIG "Marathon"

To make your **BIG DREAMS** come true, you need to **BE FIT**—physically, mentally, and emotionally. Challenge yourself to **run** 26 miles, **read** 26 books, and **do** 26 acts of kindness in 26 weeks!

RUN! 26 MILES

Try running or walking just a mile at a time. Go to DreamBigWithDave.org to get started. There you can download a printable sheet to keep track of your 26-week challenge. Check with your doctor first to make sure you're healthy and then *get moving*!

READ! 26 BOOKS

For ideas on great books for any age or interest, go to Scholastic.com. Just learning to read? Have an adult read to you. Reading chapter books? Aim for 10 pages a day or about 70 pages a week.

REACH OUT!
26 ACTS OF BIG-HEARTED KINDNESS

For a list of creative acts of kindness, check out The Joseph Middlemiss Big Heart Foundation at JMBigHeart.org. While you're there, read about Joseph's story and the amazing acts of kindness the Big Heart Foundation does.

THE FINISH LINE!

Go to DreamBigWithDave.org to find out how to get your very own *Dream Big "Marathon" Race Medal** for making it to the finish line!

*while supplies last.